NAME:

CLASS:

The **Fast Math Success: Math Word Problems Grades 2-3** is aligned with common core standards, ensuring that your child is learning the skills necessary to succeed in their academic journey. This workbook is a versatile tool that can be utilized in various educational settings, including traditional classrooms and homeschooling. It's perfect for daily math practice, homework assignments, math tests, or even as part of a 30-minute daily math routine.

Solving word problems offers numerous benefits for students. some of the key advantages include:

- ✓ **Develops critical thinking skills:** Word problems require students to analyze, evaluate and think critically about the information provided. Students learn how to break down complex problems into smaller, more manageable parts, which is a valuable skill in all areas of life.

- ✓ **Improves problem-solving abilities:** By attempting word problems, students develop a systematic approach to solving problems. They learn to identify relevant information, determine the appropriate math operation(s) and apply the correct methodology to reach a solution. These skills are essential for academic success and future careers.

- ✓ **Builds real-world connections:** Word problems offer an opportunity to apply math concepts to real-life scenarios. This helps students to understand the practical applications of math and see the relevance of what they are learning. It also helps them to develop a deeper connection with the subject matter.

- ✓ **Enhances communication skills:** Solving word problems requires students to communicate their reasoning and thought processes clearly. This helps develop their ability to articulate ideas and explain their thinking, which is a valuable skill in any profession.

- ✓ **Boosts confidence:** Successfully solving word problems can be very rewarding and help build confidence in a student's abilities. This increased self-assurance can encourage them to take on more challenging tasks and become more engaged in their education.

Encourage your child to practice word problems regularly and offer support when needed. You can also work alongside your child to apply these skills to day-to-day activities, like baking or grocery shopping.

With your encouragement and guidance, your child can improve their math skills and build a strong foundation for long-term success.

This workbook also includes answers to all the practice problems, making it easy for children to verify their work.

Copyright © 2023 SKA Books
All rights reserved. This book or any portion thereof may not be reproduced or used in any manner whatsoever without the express written permission of the publisher except for the use of brief quotations in a book review.

Contents

Addition Word Problems	**1**
Subtraction Word Problems	**27**
Multiplication Word Problems	**51**
Division Word Problems	**75**
Answers	**102**

SKA BOOKS
WITH ANSWERS
FAST MATH SUCCESS
2ND GRADE MATH WORKBOOK
SKA BOOKS

SKA BOOKS
WITH ANSWERS
GRADE 2-4
FAST MATH SUCCESS
BASIC ALGEBRA EQUATIONS WORKBOOK
SKA BOOKS

SKA BOOKS
2-3
FAST MATH SUCCESS WORKBOOK
SKA BOOKS

SKA BOOKS
WITH ANSWERS
GRADE 2-4
FAST MATH SUCCESS
ADDITION SUBTRACTION MULTIPLICATION DIVISION
SKA BOOKS

SKA BOOKS
WITH ANSWERS
GRADE 2-3
FAST MATH SUCCESS
ADDITION AND SUBTRACTION WORKBOOK
SKA BOOKS

SKA BOOKS
WITH ANSWERS
GRADE 2
FAST MATH SUCCESS
MATH CURRICULUM WORKBOOK
SKA BOOKS

Addition Word Problems

1. Nova has 31 Cakes. Her friend gives her 47 more Cakes. How many Cakes does Nova have now?

2. Luke bought 17 pencils and 26 pens. How many writing instruments did Luke buy in total?

3. There were 6 people in line at the store. After 66 more people joined the line, how many people are in the line now?

4. Christopher has a basket with 91 Highlighters in it. After buying 35 more Highlighters, how many Highlighters does Christopher have in total?

5. Madelyn has 27 papers. She gets 78 papers from her friend. How many papers does Madelyn have now?

6. Christian spent 95 dollars on Monday and 5 dollars on Tuesday. How much money did Christian spend in total?

7. A basketball team scored 9 points in the first quarter and 24 points in the second quarter. What was the total score of the basketball team after the first half?

8. Owen has 9 red marbles and 10 blue marbles in a jar. How many marbles does Owen have in total?

9. Xavier has 5 apples. He receives 10 more apples. How many apples does he have now?

10. On Monday, Jason did 29 math problems. On Tuesday, Jason did 10 more math problems. How many math problems did Jason do in total?

11. Jose has 74 apples and 4 oranges in a basket. How many fruits does Jose have in total?

12. Henry filled a tank with 93 gallons of gas and then added 2 more gallons. How many gallons of gas are in the tank now?

13. Mason had 28 dollars and earned 84 more dollars. How much money does Mason have now?

14. Michael has 97 Headphones and 68 more Headphones are added to the collection. How many Headphones does Michael have in total?

15. Ellie sold 78 Rocks on Monday and 23 Rocks on Tuesday. How many Rocks did the she sell in total?

16. At the start of the school year, there were 67 students enrolled in English class. By the end of the year, 28 more students had enrolled. How many students were enrolled in English class at the end of the year?

17. A pack of gum contains 35 pieces of gum. If 50 more pieces of gum are added to the pack, how many pieces of gum will the pack contain?

18. There are 5 cats in the ground. 63 more cats come to play. How many cats are in the ground now?

19. At the beginning of the week, there were 18 Jars in the bag. By the end of the week, 42 more Jars were added to the bag. How many Jars are in the bag now?

20. Nolan made 77 cookies and Arianna made 56 cookies. How many cookies were made in total?

21. There are 31 kids playing on the playground. 35 more kids join them. How many kids are playing now?

22. At the beginning of the week, there were 81 apples in the basket. By the end of the week, 13 more apples were added to the basket. How many apples are in the basket now?

23. Aiden has 41 notebooks. He finds 62 more notebooks. How many notebooks does he have now?

24. Josiah has 2 Wallets and buys 7 more Wallets. How many Wallets does Josiah have in total?

25. At the beginning of the day, there were 32 cups on the shelf. By the end of the day, 40 more cups were added to the shelf. How many cups are on the shelf now?

26. At the store, Robert bought 23 forks. Later, Victoria bought 75 forks from the same store. How many forks were bought in total?

27. Sadie has 69 Umbrellas. She buys 7 more Umbrellas at the store. How many Umbrellas does Sadie have now?

28. Aaron has 45 purses. His sister gives him 28 more purses. How many purses does Aaron have now?

29. Leah has 55 liters of water in a container. She pours in 16 more liters of water. How much water is in the container now?

30. The weight of an empty container is 99 pounds. If the container is filled with 23 pounds of Forks, what is the total weight of the container and its contents?

31. There are 70 bananas on the shelf. Abigail puts 25 more bananas on the shelf. How many bananas are there on the shelf now?

32. At the start of the week, 57 Coupons were in the store. By the end of the week, 5 more Coupons were added to the store. How many Coupons are in the store now?

33. Natalie has 13 Stamps in a bag. If Natalie adds 68 more Stamps to the bag, how many Stamps does Natalie have in total?

Name:

Date: __/__/____

Time Taken: ____ Min

34. Ayden has 71 red Clipboards and 60 green Clipboards. If Ayden puts all the Clipboards in a basket, how many Clipboards are in the basket in total?

35. A basket holds 20 Hairbrushes. If 47 more Hairbrushes are added to the basket, how many Hairbrushes will the basket hold in total?

36. There are 92 parrots on a tree. 63 more parrots land on the tree. How many parrots are on the tree now?

37. Isaac has 34 erasers. He buys 74 more erasers. How many erasers does she have now?

38. An object has 80 parts. If 41 more parts are added, how many parts does the object have now?

39. Leo baked 24 cookies and 81 cupcakes. How many desserts did Leo bake in total?

40. Kai has 62 dollars and found 67 more dollars on the ground. How much money does Kai have now?

41. Lily has 83 Backpacks. She buys 92 more Backpacks at the store. How many Backpacks does Lily have now?

42. Parker bought a bag of Calculators for 38 dollars. Later, Parker bought another bag of Calculators for 39 dollars. How much money did Parker spend in total?

43. Nolan had 2 dollars in the morning and earned 92 more dollars in the afternoon. How many dollars Nolan have in total?

44. James has 60 plums. He finds 29 more plums. How many plums does he have now?

45. A machine has 6 parts. If 77 more parts are added, how many parts does the machine have now?

46. There are 10 Towels in the room. 4 more Towels are brought in. How many Towels are in the room now?

47. There are 44 crows on a tree. 55 more crows land on the tree. How many crows are on the tree now?

48. There are 87 Markers in the bag. If 8 more Markers are added, how many Markers are in the bag now?

49. There are 78 trees in the garden. 77 more trees are planted. How many trees are in the garden now?

50. Xavier has 2 coins. He gets 73 more coins. How many coins does he have now?

51. Evan has 91 pencils and 42 pens. If Evan puts all the writing utensils in a case, how many writing utensils are in the case in total?

52. A bakery sold 87 cupcakes in the morning and 86 cupcakes in the afternoon. How many cupcakes did the bakery sell in total?

53. Lincoln has 49 fish in an aquarium. If Lincoln adds 61 more fish to the aquarium, how many fish will be in the aquarium in total?

54. There are 43 fishes in the pond. 96 more fishes join them. How many fishes are in the pond now?

55. Dominic has 28 Clocks. He finds 6 more Clocks on the ground. How many Clocks does Dominic have now?

56. Levi spent 6 hours studying for the history exam on Monday and 74 hours studying for the science exam on Tuesday. How many hours did Levi spend studying in total?

57. Aurora bought pizzas with 55 slices. Later, Aurora bought some more pizzas with 33 slices. How many slices of pizzas does Aurora have in total?

58. Valentina has 40 soaps. She gets 78 more soaps. How many soaps does Valentina have now?

59. Ethan has 88 Cans. He gets 19 more Cans as a gift. How many Cans does Ethan have now?

60. Luke played 5 games of chess yesterday and 21 games today. How many games of chess did Luke play in total?

61. A company produced 10 shirts on Monday and 44 shirts on Tuesday. How many shirts did the company produce in total?

62. Adam drove 56 miles in the morning and 43 miles in the evening. How many miles did Adam drive in total?

63. A soccer team scored 39 goals in the first half and 90 goals in the second half. What was the total score of the soccer team?

64. Genesis bought 21 files and later bought 79 files. How many files does Genesis have now?

65. Brody has 87 Bottles. He gets 73 more Bottles. How many Bottles does he have now?

66. A bus made 64 stops in the morning and 47 stops in the afternoon. How many stops did the bus make in total?

67. Elijah filled a tank with 81 gallons of gas and then added 89 more gallons. How many gallons of gas are in the tank now?

68. Jordan has a basket with 76 Socks in it. After buying 43 more Socks, how many Socks does Jordan have in total?

69. Isaac has 7 potatoes and 53 more potatoes are added to the collection. How many potatoes does Isaac have in total?

70. Benjamin has 91 Plates and buys 41 more Plates. How many Plates does Benjamin have in total?

71. Isabella has 51 Mirrors. She gets 65 Mirrors from her friend. How many Mirrors does Isabella have now?

72. Ryan had 2 dollars in the morning and earned 2 more dollars in the afternoon. How many dollars Ryan have in total?

73. Jayden has 73 fish in an aquarium. If Jayden adds 36 more fish to the aquarium, how many fish will be in the aquarium in total?

74. Paisley has 49 pencils in a bag. If Paisley adds 12 more pencils to the bag, how many pencils does Paisley have in total?

Subtraction Word Problems

75. There are 81 fish in a pond. Sharon caught 40 fish. How many fish are left in the pond?

76. Eric has 26 bags in his collection. He sold 24 of them at a sale. How many bags does he have left in his collection?

77. A pears costs $19 and a pen costs $15. How much more expensive is the pears than the pen?

78. There were 50 students in a class. 6 of them were absent. How many students were present in the class?

79. Donald had 94 toys. He gave 27 toys to Sharon. How many toys does Donald have left?

80. Samantha baked a 29 cookies. 18 of them were chocolate chip cookies and the rest were oatmeal raisin cookies. How many oatmeal raisin cookies did Samantha bake?

81. Daniel had 34 dollars. He spent 34 dollars on a shirts. How much money does Daniel have left?

82. James is 17 years old and Charles is 16 years old. What is the difference in their ages?

83. Jessica has 14 peaches. She gave 6 peaches to Ashley. How many peaches does Jessica have now?

84. A pizza has 96 slices. Michele ate 28 slices. How many slices of pizza are left?

85. A box of Crayons weighs 14 pounds. If you remove 11 pounds from it, how much does it weigh now?

86. Marcie bought Cameras for 67 dollars but later found out it was on sale for 34 dollars less. How much did she overpay for Cameras?

87. Ellen wants to buy coins, which costs 30 dollars. She has 8 dollars and plans to save the rest. How much more money does she need to save to buy coins?

88. Mark has 86 brushes. He traded 52 of them with his friend. How many brushes does Mark have now?

Name:

Date: __/__/____

Time Taken: ____ Min

89. Thomas saved up 25 dollars to buy papers. He spent 21 dollars on it. How much money does he have left?

90. If you have 87 bananas and you give away 73, how many bananas do you have left?

91. Samantha bought soaps for 92 dollars. She received 60 dollars in change. How much did soaps cost?

92. A cake recipe calls for 66 cups of flour. 42 cups of flour have already been added. How many more cups of flour are needed?

93. There are 2 stamps in a bag. Audrey took 1 stamp out of the bag. How many stamps are still in the bag?

94. If cell phones costs 57 dollars and you have 56 dollars, how much more money do you need to buy it?

Name: _____

Date: __/__/____

Time Taken: ____ Min

95. Jennifer has 50 potatoes. She lost 28 of them. How many potatoes does Jennifer have left?

96. There are 51 fish in a tank. If 41 leave, how many fish are left in the tank?

97. There are 37 dogs in a park. If 33 leave, how many dogs are left in the park?

98. Sharon and Deborah went shopping for clips. They had 78 dollars to spend but 61 dollars ended up being spent. How much money do they have left?

99. There are 35 plums. 31 plums are blue and the rest are red. How many red plums are in the box?

100. Emma and Sandra went on a shopping spree and bought 40 keys. After returning home, they realized that they didn't need 19 of them. How many keys did they end up keeping?

101. A small bag of chips has 10 chips in it. Andrew ate 7 chips. How many chips are left in the bag?

102. Spoons originally cost 59 dollars, but it is now on sale for 33 dollars. How much money can you save by buying it on sale?

103. Sharon has 64 Lollypops in her collection. She gave 9 of them to her friend. How many Lollypops does Sharon have now?

104. Thomas has 12 red apples and 7 green apples. How many more red apples does Thomas have than green apples?

105. A cake recipe requires 29 cups of sugar. Debra only has 20 cups of sugar. How many more cups of sugar does Debra need?

106. Ellen bought Kites for 28 dollars. She later returned some Kites and received a refund of 6 dollars. How much money did she end up spending on Kites?

107. A pack of gum had 7 pieces. Samantha took 4 pieces of gum. How many pieces of gum are left in the pack?

108. There are 3 cars in a parking lot. Donald took 1 cars out of the lot. How many cars are still in the lot?

109. Jake has 97 dollars. He wants to buy DVDs that costs 67 dollars. How much more money does he need to buy the DVDs?

110. Richard has 32 dollars. He needs to buy Rocks that costs 88 dollars. How much money will he have left after buying the Rocks?

111. There are 76 turtles in a pond. If 56 leave, how many turtles are left in the pond?

112. Deborah had 78 dollars. She spent 66 dollars on erasers. How much money does Deborah have left?

113. A box had 32 chocolates. Jessica ate 7 chocolates. How many chocolates are left in the box?

114. A recipe needs 100 cups of sugar. Karen added 90 cups of sugar. How many cups of sugar are still needed?

115. Susan and Stephanie had 67 marbles altogether. Stephanie gave 42 marbles to William. How many marbles do they have left?

116. Lemons costs 32 dollars. If you paid $9. How much change will you get back?

117. Christine has 2 dollars. She wants to buy combs, which costs 10 dollars. How much more money does she need to buy it?

118. A forks costs $70 and a pen costs $12. How much more expensive is the forks than the pen?

119. Michele and Lisa went shopping for cups. They had 96 dollars to spend but 75 dollars ended up being spent. How much money do they have left?

120. Ellen has 65 caps in her collection. She gave 58 of them to her friend. How many caps does Ellen have now?

121. A pizza has 87 slices. Sandra ate 14 slices. How many slices of pizza are left?

122. Anthony has 78 forks. He traded 2 of them with his friend. How many forks does Anthony have now?

123. There were 83 students in a class. 22 of them were absent. How many students were present in the class?

124. A small bag of chips has 85 chips in it. Paul ate 38 chips. How many chips are left in the bag?

125. A pack of gum had 99 pieces. Karen took 87 pieces of gum. How many pieces of gum are left in the pack?

126. If you have 60 bananas and you give away 16, how many bananas do you have left?

127. Jennifer wants to buy glasses, which costs 39 dollars. She has 26 dollars and plans to save the rest. How much more money does she need to save to buy glasses?

128. Erasers originally cost 42 dollars, but it is now on sale for 11 dollars. How much money can you save by buying it on sale?

129. A box had 23 chocolates. Sharon ate 7 chocolates. How many chocolates are left in the box?

130. There are 56 dogs in a park. If 23 leave, how many dogs are left in the park?

131. There are 6 fish in a pond. Sharon caught 2 fish. How many fish are left in the pond?

132. A box of clips weighs 31 pounds. If you remove 4 pounds from it, how much does it weigh now?

133. There are 74 fish in a tank. If 66 leave, how many fish are left in the tank?

134. Audrey bought cell phones for 61 dollars but later found out it was on sale for 61 dollars less. How much did she overpay for cell phones?

135. Robert had 2 dollars. He spent 1 dollars on a books. How much money does Robert have left?

136. A cake recipe requires 69 cups of sugar. Stephanie only has 18 cups of sugar. How many more cups of sugar does Stephanie need?

137. Paul has 30 red Kites and 22 green Kites. How many more red Kites does Paul have than green Kites?

138. Marin has 52 dollars. She wants to buy Cakes, which costs 53 dollars. How much more money does she need to buy it?

139. There are 26 oranges. 26 oranges are blue and the rest are red. How many red oranges are in the box?

140. Anthony saved up 92 dollars to buy Lemons. He spent 28 dollars on it. How much money does he have left?

141. Jennifer had 74 dollars. She spent 52 dollars on peaches. How much money does Jennifer have left?

142. There are 87 turtles in a pond. If 26 leave, how many turtles are left in the pond?

143. A cake recipe calls for 15 cups of flour. 15 cups of flour have already been added. How many more cups of flour are needed?

144. Linda and Barbara went on a shopping spree and bought 77 papers. After returning home, they realized that they didn't need 37 of them. How many papers did they end up keeping?

Multiplication Word Problems

145. There are 17 flowers in each bouquet. If Sophia has 16 bouquets, how many flowers does Sophia have in all?

146. There are eight pencils in each pack. If Ava buys 13 packs, how many pencils will Ava have?

147. Genesis has 15 books on each shelf, and there are four shelves. How many books does Genesis have in total?

148. Hannah has 10 boxes of apples. Each box has 15 apples. How many apples does Hannah have in all?

149. Isabella has eight jars of jam. Each jar has 12 ounces of jam. How many ounces of jam does Isabella have in all?

150. Raelynn has 19 containers of paint. Each container holds 18 liters of paint. How many liters of paint does Raelynn have in total?

151. Cooper can ride 10 miles in one hour. How far can he ride in nine hours?

152. Penelope wants to make seven pizzas, and each pizza requires 14 cups of cheese. How many cups of cheese does Penelope have?

153. Lincoln can run 11 laps in 1 hour. How many laps can Lincoln run in eight hour?

154. Levi sells 12 cakes each day at his bakery. If he works 10 days, how many cakes does he sell?

155. Brooklyn has 11 books. Each book has 20 pages. How many pages does Brooklyn have in all?

156. There are six pages in a book. If 12 books are needed for a class, how many pages are there in total?

157. A box contains 12 bottles of juice, and each bottle contains 13 ounces of juice. How many ounces of juice are there in total?

158. Andrew can lift 16 pounds of weight. How many pounds of weight can he lift in three repetitions?

159. If a bicycle travels at eight miles per hour for three hours, how far will it go?

160. A bookshelf can hold three books. If there are 19 bookshelves in a room, how many books can the room hold in total?

161. If there are 16 students in each classroom and there are eight classrooms, how many students are there in total?

162. A recipe for a cake calls for eight cups of flour. How many cups of flour are needed to make four cakes?

163. There are eight Crayons in each bag. If Addison buys six bags, how many Crayons will Addison have?

164. There are nine seats on a bus. If eight buses are needed to transport a group of people, how many people can the group consist of at most?

165. Piper baked 12 batches of cakes. Each batch had 13 cakes. How many cakes did Piper bake in all?

166. Maverick can solve 14 math problems in one hour. How many math problems can Maverick solve in 19 hours?

167. Genesis baked seven batches of cookies. Each batch had 11 cookies. How many cookies did Genesis bake in all?

168. If a train travels at 15 miles per hour for 12 hours, how far will it go?

169. Diego runs 11 miles per week. How many miles will Diego run in five weeks?

170. A garden has 10 rows of flowers and four flowers in each row. How many flowers are there in total?

171. Savannah has seven yards of fabric, and each dress requires 20 yards of fabric. How many dresses can Savannah make?

172. Easton can make 20 sandwiches in 1 hour. How many sandwiches can he make in 17 hour?

173. Emma has 12 vases of flowers. Each vase has 17 flowers. How many flowers does Emma have in all?

174. There are three students in a class. If each student needs four pencils, how many pencils are needed for the class in total?

175. William can solve nine math problems in one hour. How many problems can William solve in nine hours?

176. Alexander can do eight pushups in one minute. How many pushups can Alexander do in six minutes?

177. Gabriel can catch 10 fish per hour. How many fish can Gabriel catch in two hours?

Name:

Date:
__/__/____

Time Taken:
____ Min

178. If a boat travels at three miles per hour for four hours, how far will it go?

179. There are three bananas in each bunch. If Paisley buys four bunches, how many bananas will Paisley have?

180. Thomas can type eight words per minute. How many words can Thomas type in seven minutes?

181. Kingston can lift 20 pounds of weight. How many pounds of weight can Kingston lift in total if he lifts for five sets?

182. There are 18 shelves in Nicholas's bookcase. 18 books can fit on each shelf. How many books can the bookcase hold in total?

183. Evan runs eight miles every day. How many miles will Evan run in seven days?

184. Sebastian earns six dollars per hour. How much will Sebastian earn after working for two hours?

185. If a car travels at 19 miles per hour for six hours, how far will it go?

186. There are 12 shelves in a library. Five books can fit on each shelf. How many books the library have in total?

187. There are 14 slices of pizza in each box. If Jordyn orders 20 boxes, how many slices of pizza will Jordyn have?

188. Leo can lift 13 kilograms of weight. How many kilograms of weight can he lift in 17 lifts?

189. If Joseph can paint nine square feet of wall in one hour, how many square feet of wall can he paint in 11 hours?

190. Amelia wants to make 13 flower arrangements, and each arrangement requires 12 flowers. How many flowers does Amelia need in total?

191. A movie theater can seat five people. How many people can it seat in seven showings?

192. There are 20 cars in a parking lot. If each car needs five liters of gasoline, how many liters of gasoline are needed for all the cars?

193. Daniel can ride seven miles in one hour. How far can he ride in nine hours?

194. There are 11 cars in a parking lot. If each car needs seven liters of gasoline, how many liters of gasoline are needed for all the cars?

195. Emilia baked nine batches of cookies. Each batch had 12 cookies. How many cookies did Emilia bake in all?

196. There are 10 shelves in David's bookcase. Eight books can fit on each shelf. How many books can the bookcase hold in total?

197. Paisley has 17 vases of flowers. Each vase has five flowers. How many flowers does Paisley have in all?

198. Alexander runs five miles every day. How many miles will Alexander run in four days?

199. Amelia has three boxes of Keychains. Each box has three Keychains. How many Keychains does Amelia have in all?

200. Harper has 11 yards of fabric, and each dress requires six yards of fabric. How many dresses can Harper make?

201. There are 12 pencils in each pack. If Peyton buys two packs, how many pencils will Peyton have?

202. Natalie has five containers of paint. Each container holds four liters of paint. How many liters of paint does Natalie have in total?

203. There are 17 slices of pizza in each box. If Sofia orders five boxes, how many slices of pizza will Sofia have?

204. Miles can type 12 words per minute. How many words can Miles type in 11 minutes?

205. A recipe for a cake calls for 10 cups of flour. How many cups of flour are needed to make seven cakes?

206. A box contains 16 bottles of juice, and each bottle contains 13 ounces of juice. How many ounces of juice are there in total?

207. There are 12 pages in a book. If 17 books are needed for a class, how many pages are there in total?

208. Camila baked three batches of cakes. Each batch had 14 cakes. How many cakes did Camila bake in all?

209. There are six Calculators in each bag. If Addison buys 15 bags, how many Calculators will Addison have?

210. There are 13 bananas in each bunch. If Aubrey buys 19 bunches, how many bananas will Aubrey have?

211. Genesis wants to make 17 flower arrangements, and each arrangement requires 20 flowers. How many flowers does Genesis need in total?

212. Grayson can lift 13 pounds of weight. How many pounds of weight can Grayson lift in total if he lifts for eight sets?

213. Bentley runs 16 miles per week. How many miles will Bentley run in six weeks?

214. Victoria has eight books on each shelf, and there are 10 shelves. How many books does Victoria have in total?

215. If Christopher can paint 16 square feet of wall in one hour, how many square feet of wall can he paint in 10 hours?

216. If a train travels at 15 miles per hour for seven hours, how far will it go?

Division Word Problems

217. If a store sells 14 Hairbrushes for $280 how much will each Hairbrushes cost?

218. At a restaurant, 19 friends decided to divide the bill equally. If each person paid $nine, then what was the total bill?

219. A box contains 196 candy bars. If each candy bar has 14 calories, how many calories are there in the box?

220. Leah bought four Forks for a total of $20. How much did each Forks cost?

221. A recipe calls for 132 cups of sugar to make 11 cookies. How much sugar is needed to make 1 cookie?

222. Liam has 130 dollars and wants to buy 10 Staplers. How much can he spend on each Staplers?

223. If a box contains 204 chocolates and each person can have 12 chocolates, how many people can be served from that box?

224. How many 10 cm pieces of rope can you cut from a rope that is 50 cm long?

225. A box of bottles has 72 bottles. If 18 children each get an equal number of bottles, how many bottles will each child get?

226. Genesis has $81 and she wants to buy nine Plates that cost the same amount. How much does each Plates cost?

227. A pool is 20 meters long. If it is divided into five equal parts, how long is each part?

228. How many 17 cm pieces of pipe can you cut from a pipe that is 238 cm long?

229. If the pizzas have 45 slices and is divided equally among 15 people, how many slices will each person get?

230. Brandon is reading a book with 70 pages. If Brandon wants to read the same number of pages every day, how many pages would Brandon have to read each day to finish in seven days?

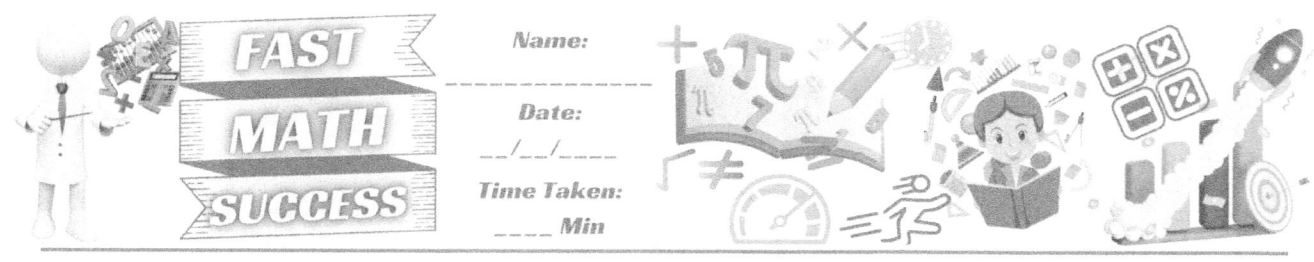

231. A box of Diapers weighs 85 pounds. If one Diaper weighs five pounds, how many Diapers are there in the box?

232. Madelyn made 240 cookies for a bake sale. She put the cookies in bags, with 16 cookies in each bag. How many bags did she have for the bake sale?

233. If Charlotte has six coins and wants to distribute them equally to two students, how many coins will each student get?

234. If Owen has 108 books and wants to share them equally among six friends, how many books will each friend get?

235. If Eva has 65 cups and wants to divide them equally among five friends, how many cups will each friend get?

236. Piper is packing 135 cupcakes into boxes. Each box can hold 15 cupcakes. How many boxes will Piper need?

237. Brody drove 208 miles in 13 hours. What was Brody's average speed in miles per hour?

238. A rope is 10 meters long. If you cut it into two equal pieces, how long is each piece?

239. Anthony has 102 pages of homework to do. If he wants to finish his homework in 17 days, how many pages does he need to do each day?

240. A roll of tape is 49 feet long. If Luna needs to cut the tape into seven pieces that are all the same length, how long will each piece be?

241. Peyton has 68 Calculators and wants to divide them equally among 17 children. How many Calculators will each child get?

242. Paisley can run 153 miles in 17 hours. How many miles can she run in 1 hour?

243. If a garden is 306 feet wide and it is divided into 18 equal parts, how wide is each part?

244. Everly is filling up water bottles. Each bottle holds four ounces of water. If Everly has 44 ounces of water, how many water bottles can she fill up?

245. If a box contains 35 Crayons and each person can have five Crayons, how many people can be served from that box?

246. If a garden is 195 feet long and it is divided into 15 equal parts, how long is each part?

247. Joshua read a book that had 126 pages in nine days. If he read the same number of pages each day, how many pages did he read per day?

248. A car can travel 30 miles on two gallons of gas. How many miles can it travel on 1 gallon of gas?

249. Molly has 255 Jackets. If Molly divides them evenly among 17 children, how many Jackets will each child get?

250. You have 132 clips and want to share them equally with 12 people. How many clips would each person get?

251. If a field is 169 acres and it is divided into 13 equal parts, how many acres is each part?

252. If Evelyn has 120 pens and wants to distribute them equally to 20 students, how many pens will each student get?

253. If a rope is 180 meters long and you want to cut it into nine equal pieces, how long will each piece be?

254. Sebastian can type 153 words in 17 minutes. How many words can he type in 1 minute?

255. Bella baked 52 cakes for a party. If she wants to divide them into four equal portions, how many cakes will each portion have?

256. Aria has 170 files and wants to divide them equally among 17 people. How many files will each person get?

257. Jade has 320 cookies and wants to divide them equally into 16 bags. How many cookies will be in each bag?

258. Ayden scored 28 points in 14 games. What is his average score per game?

259. It takes Violet eight minutes to write 1 page. How many pages can Violet write in 160 minutes?

260. A book has 108 chapters. If you want to read the book in 18 days, how many chapters do you need to read per day?

261. Daniel scored 300 points in 20 games. What is his average score per game?

262. At a restaurant, 14 friends decided to divide the bill equally. If each person paid $19, then what was the total bill?

263. Natalie has 72 Towels. If Natalie divides them evenly among 18 children, how many Towels will each child get?

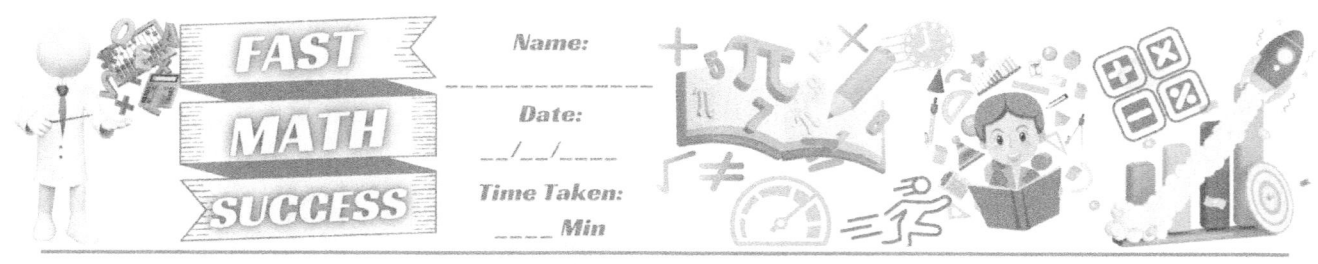

264. Ellie is filling up water bottles. Each bottle holds two ounces of water. If Ellie has 38 ounces of water, how many water bottles can she fill up?

265. How many 16 cm pieces of rope can you cut from a rope that is 112 cm long?

266. Dominic read a book that had 27 pages in nine days. If he read the same number of pages each day, how many pages did he read per day?

267. A pool is 238 meters long. If it is divided into 14 equal parts, how long is each part?

268. If Ellie has 75 mangoes and wants to divide them equally among 15 friends, how many mangoes will each friend get?

269. Natalie has 60 pencils and wants to divide them equally among five people. How many pencils will each person get?

270. If a field is 36 acres and it is divided into two equal parts, how many acres is each part?

271. A rope is 300 meters long. If you cut it into 20 equal pieces, how long is each piece?

272. If a rope is 104 meters long and you want to cut it into eight equal pieces, how long will each piece be?

273. A recipe calls for 60 cups of sugar to make 10 cookies. How much sugar is needed to make 1 cookie?

274. Gemma has 153 notebooks and wants to divide them equally among 17 children. How many notebooks will each child get?

275. If Camila has four pens and wants to distribute them equally to two students, how many pens will each student get?

276. It takes Olivia 10 minutes to write 1 page. How many pages can Olivia write in 150 minutes?

277. Jade made 126 cookies for a bake sale. She put the cookies in bags, with 18 cookies in each bag. How many bags did she have for the bake sale?

278. If a box contains 198 chocolates and each person can have 11 chocolates, how many people can be served from that box?

279. How many 19 cm pieces of pipe can you cut from a pipe that is 38 cm long?

280. If the pizzas have 56 slices and is divided equally among eight people, how many slices will each person get?

281. A box of Cans weighs 360 pounds. If one Can weighs 20 pounds, how many Cans are there in the box?

282. A box contains 238 candy bars. If each candy bar has 14 calories, how many calories are there in the box?

283. Savannah is packing 80 cupcakes into boxes. Each box can hold five cupcakes. How many boxes will Savannah need?

284. If a garden is 340 feet wide and it is divided into 17 equal parts, how wide is each part?

285. If a garden is 60 feet long and it is divided into six equal parts, how long is each part?

286. Jackson is reading a book with 153 pages. If Jackson wants to read the same number of pages every day, how many pages would Jackson have to read each day to finish in 17 days?

287. A car can travel 160 miles on eight gallons of gas. How many miles can it travel on 1 gallon of gas?

288. Stella bought six keys for a total of $36. How much did each keys cost?

289. A box of Lemons has 24 Lemons. If eight children each get an equal number of Lemons, how many Lemons will each child get?

290. If a box contains 140 potatoes and each person can have 10 potatoes, how many people can be served from that box?

ANSWERS

Page 1: Addition Word Problems

1. 78 2. 43 3. 72 4. 126 5. 105 6. 100 7. 33
8. 19 9. 15 10. 39 11. 78 12. 95 13. 112 14. 165
15. 101 16. 95 17. 85 18. 68 19. 60 20. 133 21. 66
22. 94 23. 103 24. 9 25. 72 26. 98 27. 76 28. 73
29. 71 30. 122 31. 95 32. 62 33. 81 34. 131 35. 67
36. 155 37. 108 38. 121 39. 105 40. 129 41. 175 42. 77
43. 94 44. 89 45. 83 46. 14 47. 99 48. 95 49. 155
50. 75 51. 133 52. 173 53. 110 54. 139 55. 34 56. 80
57. 88 58. 118 59. 107 60. 26 61. 54 62. 99 63. 129
64. 100 65. 160 66. 111 67. 170 68. 119 69. 60 70. 132
71. 116 72. 4 73. 109 74. 61

Page 27: Subtraction Word Problems

75. 41 76. 2 77. 4 78. 44 79. 67 80. 11 81. 0
82. 1 83. 8 84. 68 85. 3 86. 33 87. 22 88. 34
89. 4 90. 14 91. 32 92. 24 93. 1 94. 1 95. 22

96. 10	97. 4	98. 17	99. 4	100. 21	101. 3	102. 26
103. 55	104. 5	105. 9	106. 22	107. 3	108. 2	109. 30
110. 56	111. 20	112. 12	113. 25	114. 10	115. 25	116. 23
117. 8	118. 58	119. 21	120. 7	121. 73	122. 76	123. 61
124. 47	125. 12	126. 44	127. 13	128. 31	129. 16	130. 33
131. 4	132. 27	133. 8	134. 0	135. 1	136. 51	137. 8
138. 1	139. 0	140. 64	141. 22	142. 61	143. 0	144. 40

Page 51: Multiplication Word Problems

145. 272	146. 104	147. 60	148. 150	149. 96	150. 342
151. 90	152. 98	153. 88	154. 120	155. 220	156. 72
157. 156	158. 48	159. 24	160. 57	161. 128	162. 32
163. 48	164. 72	165. 156	166. 266	167. 77	168. 180
169. 55	170. 40	171. 140	172. 340	173. 204	174. 12
175. 81	176. 48	177. 20	178. 12	179. 12	180. 56
181. 100	182. 324	183. 56	184. 12	185. 114	186. 60
187. 280	188. 221	189. 99	190. 156	191. 35	192. 100
193. 63	194. 77	195. 108	196. 80	197. 85	198. 20

199. 9   200. 66   201. 24   202. 20   203. 85   204. 132
205. 70   206. 208   207. 204   208. 42   209. 90   210. 247
211. 340   212. 104   213. 96   214. 80   215. 160   216. 105

Page 75: Division Word Problems

217. 20   218. 171   219. 14   220. 5   221. 12   222. 13
223. 17   224. 5   225. 4   226. 9   227. 4   228. 14
229. 3   230. 10   231. 17   232. 15   233. 3   234. 18
235. 13   236. 9   237. 16   238. 5   239. 6   240. 7
241. 4   242. 9   243. 17   244. 11   245. 7   246. 13
247. 14   248. 15   249. 15   250. 11   251. 13   252. 6
253. 20   254. 9   255. 13   256. 10   257. 20   258. 2
259. 20   260. 6   261. 15   262. 266   263. 4   264. 19
265. 7   266. 3   267. 17   268. 5   269. 12   270. 18
271. 15   272. 13   273. 6   274. 9   275. 2   276. 15
277. 7   278. 18   279. 2   280. 7   281. 18   282. 17
283. 16   284. 20   285. 10   286. 9   287. 20   288. 6
289. 3   290. 14

Made in United States
North Haven, CT
27 March 2025